TECHNICAL REPORT

T0097114

The Effects of the Changes in Chapter 7 Debtors' Lien-Avoidance Rights Under the Bankruptcy Abuse Prevention and Consumer Protection Act of 2005

Stephen J. Carroll, Noreen Clancy, Melissa A. Bradley, Jennifer Pevar, P. Jane McClure

Prepared for the Executive Office for U.S. Trustees

RAND INSTITUTE FOR CIVIL JUSTICE

The research described in this report was prepared for the Executive Office for U.S. Trustees by the RAND Institute for Civil Justice.

Library of Congress Cataloging-in-Publication Data

The effects of the changes in Chapter 7 debtors' lien-avoidance rights under the Bankruptcy Abuse Prevention and Consumer Protection Act of 2005 / Stephen J. Carroll ... [et al.].
    p. cm.
    ISBN 978-0-8330-4207-1 (pbk. : alk. paper)
    1. Bankruptcy—United States. 2. United States. Bankruptcy Abuse Prevention and Consumer Protection Act of 2005. 3. Debtor and creditor—United States. 4. Consumer protection—Law and legislation—United States. 5. Consumer credit—Law and legislation—United States. I. Carroll, Stephen J., 1940–

KF1525.E34 2007
346.7307'8—dc22

                                                                    2007030767

The RAND Corporation is a nonprofit research organization providing objective analysis and effective solutions that address the challenges facing the public and private sectors around the world. RAND's publications do not necessarily reflect the opinions of its research clients and sponsors.

RAND® is a registered trademark.

Published 2007 by the RAND Corporation
1776 Main Street, P.O. Box 2138, Santa Monica, CA 90407-2138
1200 South Hayes Street, Arlington, VA 22202-5050
4570 Fifth Avenue, Suite 600, Pittsburgh, PA 15213-2665
RAND URL: http://www.rand.org/
To order RAND documents or to obtain additional information, contact
Distribution Services: Telephone: (310) 451-7002;
Fax: (310) 451-6915; Email: order@rand.org

Preface

The Bankruptcy Abuse Prevention and Consumer Protection Act of 2005 (BAPCPA) changed debtors' lien-avoidance rights. The RAND Corporation conducted qualitative and quantitative analyses to estimate the impact of BAPCPA's new definition of *household goods* on debtors and whether debtor behavior signaled a change in creditors' business practices. The analyses addressed questions about how changes in the types of exempt household goods on which liens can be avoided may have induced changes in the fraction of household goods claimed as exempt, in the fraction of household goods pledged as collateral for loans, and in the distribution of debtors' intentions regarding household goods pledged as collateral.

This research was sponsored by the Executive Office for U.S. Trustees (EOUST), whose mission is to promote the integrity and efficiency of the U.S. bankruptcy system. This report should be of interest to state and federal policymakers concerned with bankruptcy issues. It should also be of interest to bankruptcy practitioners and the credit industry.

The RAND Institute for Civil Justice

The mission of the RAND Institute for Civil Justice (ICJ) is to improve private and public decisionmaking on civil legal issues by supplying policymakers and the public with the results of objective, empirically based, analytic research. ICJ facilitates change in the civil justice system by analyzing trends and outcomes, identifying and evaluating policy options, and bringing together representatives of different interests to debate alternative solutions to policy problems. ICJ builds on a long tradition of RAND research characterized by an interdisciplinary, empirical approach to public policy issues and rigorous standards of quality, objectivity, and independence.

ICJ research is supported by pooled grants from corporations, trade and professional associations, and individuals; by government grants and contracts; and by private foundations. ICJ disseminates its work widely to the legal, business, and research communities and to the general public. In accordance with RAND policy, all ICJ research products are subject to peer review before publication. ICJ publications do not necessarily reflect the opinions or policies of the research sponsors or of the ICJ Board of Overseers.

Information about ICJ is available online (http://www.rand.org/icj/). Inquiries about research projects should be sent to the following address:

Robert T. Reville, Director
RAND Institute for Civil Justice
1776 Main Street
P.O. Box 2138
Santa Monica, CA 90407-2138
310-393-0411 x6786
Fax: 310-451-6979
Robert_Reville@rand.org

Contents

Tables

Summary

The Bankruptcy Abuse Prevention and Consumer Protection Act of 2005 (BAPCPA) limited the types and quantities of exempt household goods on which debtors could avoid certain liens. Part of the motivation for these changes was a perception that debtors were using their household goods as collateral to obtain loans that they never intended to repay. The perception was that debtors intended from the outset to file for bankruptcy and avoid the nonpossessory, nonpurchase money lien and then avoid the debt.[1]

There was some concern that BAPCPA may have induced changes in the use of nonpossessory, nonpurchase money security liens. Debtors might have become less willing to obtain loans secured by a nonpossessory, nonpurchase money lien because surrendering the assets cannot be avoided in a subsequent bankruptcy. Alternatively, lenders might have become more willing to give loans using nonpossessory, nonpurchase money liens knowing that the liens on certain items can no longer be avoided. The U.S. Congress directed the Executive Office for U.S. Trustees (EOUST) to examine the effects of the changes in debtors' lien avoidance rights (BAPCPA, §313[b]). EOUST, in turn, asked the RAND Corporation to examine whether there had been a change in business practices associated with a debtor's right to avoid a nonpossessory, nonpurchase money lien on household goods (e.g., whether the amounts and types of loans secured by debtors' household goods have changed since BAPCPA).

We conducted both qualitative and quantitative research to assess the effects of the new definition of the types and quantities of household goods exempt from certain liens. We interviewed bankruptcy attorneys, judges, trustees, creditors, and U.S. trustee (UST) office staff as to whether they are seeing any changes related to the new limits on lien avoidance for household goods. We consistently heard that no one is noticing any changes in debtor or creditor behavior due to the new definition of *household goods*. Some interview participants noted that it may be too early to tell whether businesses are changing their practices related to this issue.

Our quantitative research seems to support the view that not much has changed due to the new limits on lien avoidance for household goods. We drew a sample of 100 Chapter 7 bankruptcy cases (50 pre-BAPCPA and 50 post-BAPCPA) from each of eight judicial districts. For pre- and post-BAPCPA filers, we compared the debtors' financial characteristics (such as personal property, household goods, assets, and liabilities), the amounts and frequencies of loans secured with the BAPCPA-affected goods, and debtors' intentions regarding disposition of debts secured with such goods.

---

[1] *Nonpossessory, nonpurchase money* means that the debtor owned the asset against which the lien was taken before using the asset as collateral for debt and that the creditor did not take possession of the asset as security for the debt.

We found no significant difference in the general financial characteristics of Chapter 7 debtors filing pre- and post-BAPCPA. Given the wide variability in debtor financial characteristics, however, this lack of significance may be due to insufficient statistical power. Although we cannot make any conclusions regarding actual changes, we did see a noticeable drop in the amount of the average Chapter 7 debtor's real property and secured debts.

With respect to BAPCPA-specific effects, we cannot draw any conclusions. Although we had an overall sample size of 800 (400 pre- and 400 post-BAPCPA), only about 10 percent of these cases (36 pre-BAPCPA and 42 post-BAPCPA) had a loan potentially secured with BAPCPA-affected goods.[2] Of these, we could not determine from the information contained in the debtor schedules whether the loans were possessory or nonpossessory. As a result, it was impossible to conduct any meaningful statistical analysis about BAPCPA's effect either from the secured-loan information or debtors' intentions regarding such loans. The only conclusion we can draw from the data we collected is that, based on our sample, even before BAPCPA was enacted, it appears that debtors seldom used BAPCPA-affected goods to secure loans (either possessory or nonpossessory) and attempted to use a lien-avoidance provision for such loans even less frequently (in fewer than 1 percent of the filings). This is not surprising, given that items on which it is even legal to take a nonpossessory, nonpurchase security interest—antiques, works of art and jewelry (other than wedding rings)—are ones that most Chapter 7 debtors do not even own.

---

[2]   From the cases, we could not determine the exact nature of the goods that were used to secure these loans, so we had to use proxies for BAPCPA-affected goods.

Acknowledgments

We would like to thank Marianne Culhane and Michaela White of Creighton University School of Law, who served as consultants on this study. Their knowledge of the inner workings of the bankruptcy process proved extremely helpful as we devised a research approach to assess any changes by debtors or creditors in relation to the definition of *household goods*. They were also helpful sounding boards throughout our data collection and analysis processes. We would like to thank all of those who participated in the interviews and took the time to convey their practical experiences. We would also like to thank Katie Smythe of RAND, who helped us conduct many of the interviews and provided helpful comments on drafts of this report. Comments by our reviewers, Elaine Reardon of RAND and Katherine Porter of the University of Iowa College of Law, increased the quality and clarity of this study.

Abbreviations

BAPCPA	Bankruptcy Abuse Prevention and Consumer Protection Act of 2005
EOUST	Executive Office for U.S. Trustees
ICJ	RAND Institute for Civil Justice
MDI	monthly disposable income
UST	U.S. trustee
USTP	U.S. Trustee Program

CHAPTER ONE

Introduction

On April 20, 2005, President George W. Bush signed the Bankruptcy Abuse Prevention and Consumer Protection Act of 2005 (BAPCPA). The act took effect October 17, 2005. BAPCPA imposed new limits on debtors' rights to avoid liens on exempt personal property. Specifically, BAPCPA provides a new definition of the types and quantities of personal property that constitute household goods for lien avoidance under section 522(f) of the Bankruptcy Code.[1] The changes were designed to halt a perceived abuse in that some debtors would use their avoidance rights to keep property that they had pledged as collateral for nonpossessory, nonpurchase money loans.[2] The text box on the following page lists the household goods subject to lien avoidance pre-BAPCPA (§522[f][B]). It also shows the more specific definition of *household goods* introduced by BAPCPA and the types of household goods that are excluded from lien avoidance (§522[f][4][A] and [B]).

At the time of passage, some voiced concern that the change in the specification of the household goods that qualify for lien-avoidance actions may induce changes in business practices associated with a debtor's right to avoid nonpossessory, nonpurchase money liens. Lenders may have become more willing to take certain household goods as collateral, safe in the knowledge that the lien will not be avoided. As a result, debtors, who are supposed to have a fresh start following bankruptcy, may be strong-armed into unnecessary reaffirmations by unscrupulous creditors.

These fears led the U.S. Congress to require the director of the Executive Office for U.S. Trustees (EOUST) to examine the use of the definition of *household goods* and the impact of section 522(f)(4) on debtors and the bankruptcy courts. The specific language from BAPCPA reads as follows:

> (b) STUDY—Not later than 2 years after the date of enactment of this Act, the Director of the Executive Office for United States Trustees shall submit a report to the Committee on the Judiciary of the Senate and the Committee on the Judiciary of the House of Representatives containing its findings regarding the utilization of the definition of household goods, as defined in section 522(f)(4) of title 11, United States Code, as added by subsection (a), with respect to the avoidance of nonpossessory, nonpurchase money security

---

[1] Specifically, §522(f)(4)(A) and §522(f)(1)(B)(i) contained in §313(a) of BAPCPA. Using the law as a guide, we use the general term *household goods* throughout this report when referring to personal property subject to lien avoidance.

[2] A *purchase-money security interest* is a lien on property purchased on credit and pledged as collateral for the loan. If a debtor pledges property that he or she already owned as collateral on a loan and retains possession of the property rather than giving the property to the lender (e.g., a pawn broker), the lien is a nonpossessory, nonpurchase money security interest.

Household Goods Subject to Lien Avoidance Pre-BAPCPA (11 U.S.C. 522[f][B])

The Bankruptcy Code (11 U.S.C §522[f][B]) lists the household goods subject to lien avoidance pre-BAPCPA. BAPCPA further defines the term *household goods* by adding subsection (f)(4)(A) and by excluding certain items from the list of household goods subject to lien avoidance (f)(4)(B).

Section 522(f)(B) a nonpossessory, nonpurchase-money security interest in any—(i) household furnishings, household goods, wearing apparel, appliances, books, animals, crops, musical instruments, or jewelry that are held primarily for the personal, family, or household use of the debtor or a dependent of the debtor; (ii) implements, professional books, or tools, of the trade of the debtor or the trade of a dependent of the debtor; or (iii) professionally prescribed health aids for the debtor or a dependent of the debtor.

BAPCPA added the following to §522(f)

Section 522(f) of title 11, United States Code, is amended by adding at the end the following:

(4)(A) Subject to subparagraph (B), for purposes of paragraph (1)(B), the term "household goods" means—(i) clothing; (ii) furniture; (iii) appliances; (iv) 1 radio; (v) 1 television; (vi) 1 VCR; (vii) linens; (viii) china; (ix) crockery; (x) kitchenware; (xi) educational materials and educational equipment primarily for the use of minor dependent children of the debtor; (xii) medical equipment and supplies; (xiii) furniture exclusively for the use of minor children, or elderly or disabled dependents of the debtor; (xiv) personal effects (including the toys and hobby equipment of minor dependent children and wedding rings) of the debtor and the dependents of the debtor; and (xv) 1 personal computer and related equipment.

(B) The term "household goods" does not include—(i) works of art (unless by or of the debtor, or any relative of the debtor); (ii) electronic entertainment equipment with a fair market value of more than $500 in the aggregate (except 1 television, 1 radio, and 1 VCR); (iii) items acquired as antiques with a fair market value of more than $500 in the aggregate; (iv) jewelry with a fair market value of more than $500 in the aggregate (except wedding rings); and (v) a computer (except as otherwise provided for in this section), motor vehicle (including a tractor or lawn tractor), boat, or a motorized recreational device, conveyance, vehicle, watercraft, or aircraft.

interests in household goods under section 522(f)(1)(B) of title 11, United States Code, and the impact such section 522(f)(4) has had on debtors and the bankruptcy courts. Such report may include recommendation for amendments to such section 522(f)(4) consistent with the Director's findings. (Public Law 109-8, section 313b)

EOUST, in turn, asked RAND to examine whether there had been a change in business practices associated with a debtor's right to avoid a nonpossessory, nonpurchase money lien on household goods. We conducted qualitative and quantitative analyses to assess the effects of the new definition of the types and quantities of household goods on which liens can be avoided. We conducted interviews and group discussions with informed individuals and government employees involved in the bankruptcy process to elucidate issues and patterns. We examined samples of bankruptcy cases filed in eight judicial districts to empirically estimate the new definition's effects on debtors. This report presents the results of these analyses.

Background

One of the principal goals of bankruptcy is to grant debtors a fresh start so that they may become productive members of society on emergence from bankruptcy. Bankruptcy affords property exemptions to debtors to ensure that they can emerge from bankruptcy not only free of debt but also with some necessary assets. Property exemptions are designed to provide the debtor with the basic necessities so the debtor is not a ward of society after bankruptcy.

In addition to personal-property exemptions, Congress fashioned another protection to improve the economic position of postbankruptcy debtors: permission to avoid liens on some exempt property so that it would not be repossessed. There were concerns that some creditors were using security interests to take advantage of the poor. These creditors took security interests in a debtor's clothing, family photographs, and other household items. Critics thought that these security interests were not taken in the belief that the collateral could be sold to repay the loan if the debtor became unable to pay, but that they were taken because of the collateral's emotional value to the debtor, who would presumably make any sacrifice to find a way to pay and thus retain those goods.

The Bankruptcy Code permits avoidance of judicial liens and some voluntary security interests on some otherwise exempt items. Specifically, nonpossessory, nonpurchase money security interests in exempt household furnishings, wearing apparel, tools of the trade,[3] and professionally prescribed health aids can be avoided in bankruptcy. Creditors who had these security interests or liens were treated as unsecured creditors, entitled only to a pro rata share of the debtor's estate.

Enactment in 1978 of the Bankruptcy Code provision allowing lien avoidance on exempt property led to the adoption of an FTC rule[4] imposing similar restraints outside bankruptcy. The debate over this provision drew widespread attention to industry practices involving nonpossessory, nonpurchase money security interests. Perceived creditor abuses were widely noted, and the Bankruptcy Code provision was seen as an important consumer protection. In response to the consumer-protection concerns and to avoid incentives to file for bankruptcy, the FTC adopted a rule making it an unfair trade practice for a company to take a nonpossessory, nonpurchase money security interest in a specified list of goods.

But with the protections afforded debtors under the Bankruptcy Code with respect to nonpossessory, nonpurchase money security interests came concern that debtors were now

---

[3] The purpose of the lien avoidance in household goods is similar to the purpose of capping lien avoidance for tools of the trade and farm animals. Several years before the enactment of BAPCPA, Congress tightened the tools-of-the-trade lien-avoidance power when it became apparent that it was being abused to avoid liens on expensive tractors and other high-end "tools" or to protect racehorses as "farm animals" that qualify for the "pet" exception. See §522(f)(3)(B) (capping lien avoidance at $5,000 in some situations).

[4] 16 CFR 444.1–444.5; definition of *household goods* is in 444.1 I.

abusing the process. Bankruptcy Court decisions prior to the enactment of BAPCPA often interpreted the definition of *household goods* so broadly that debtors were allowed to avoid such liens, even on goods not covered by the FTC rule. Thus, the chance to avoid more liens in bankruptcy than one could avoid outside of bankruptcy provided an incentive to file, especially for wealthier debtors. In response to this concern, BAPCPA modified the definition of *household goods*, narrowing the avoidance to more closely match the definition applied by the FTC under its credit-practices rule. Specifically, BAPCPA prevents lien avoidance on most electronic equipment (a debtor can keep one radio, one television, one VCR, and one computer with related equipment), most works of art, jewelry (except for wedding rings), and antiques worth more than $500. It is reasonable to expect that these changes will encourage consistency in court interpretations and reduce litigation.

Having enacted these changes, Congress now seeks to determine what impact, if any, the narrowed category of household goods subject to lien avoidance has had on debtors and on bankruptcy courts. To study this issue, we attempted to address the following research questions using interviews and data from a broad, generalizable sample of debtors.

Research Questions

The effects of business practices associated with a debtor's right to avoid a lien on household goods will be reflected in the amounts and frequencies of loans secured with household goods and in the frequency with which debtors seek to avoid liens on loans secured with household goods. Because changes in the average debtor's financial characteristics could affect these outcomes, we explored patterns in debtors' financial circumstances before and after BAPCPA took effect. Accordingly, the analysis of the effects of the new definition of *household goods* provided by BAPCPA focused on three questions:

1. Have the average debtor's general financial characteristics changed from before to after BAPCPA enactment?
2. Has there been a significant change in the amount or frequency of loans secured with household goods by the average debtor from before to after BAPCPA enactment?
3. Has the distribution of debtors' intentions regarding household goods pledged as collateral for a secured, nonpossessory, nonpurchase money loan changed from before to after BAPCPA enactment?

Have the Average Debtor's General Financial Characteristics Changed from Before to After BAPCPA Enactment?

Prior to BAPCPA, some debtors in financial straits may have secured loans using household goods as collateral in the expectation that if, or when, they filed for bankruptcy, these goods would be declared exempt and they could keep the goods while their debts were avoided. In fact, as noted previously, this possibility was a motivating factor in the modification of this portion of BAPCPA. To the extent that debtors were so motivated, the new definition would have eliminated the incentive to secure loans with household goods on which a lien could no longer be avoided under the narrowed category of household goods subject to lien avoidance.

To distill the impact, if any, of changes due to BAPCPA, we first explored the average debtor's general financial characteristics both before and after BAPCPA was enacted to determine whether there were any significant changes.

Has There Been a Significant Change in the Amount or Frequency of Loans Secured with Household Goods by the Average Debtor from Before to After BAPCPA Enactment?

Part of the motivation behind BAPCPA was a perception that debtors were using their household goods as security to obtain loans that they never intended to repay. Instead, debtors filed for bankruptcy and used the nonpossessory, nonpurchase money lien-avoidance provision in bankruptcy law to avoid the debt. If true, we would expect a reduction in the amount and frequency of secured loans on household goods, since BAPCPA significantly limited debtors' incentive to engage in this behavior.

However, debtors may be motivated by financial need rather than by the potential benefits of bankruptcy provisions. Under this scenario, debtors do not use their household goods to obtain loans because they think the debt can be avoided in a subsequent bankruptcy. Rather, using these goods as collateral to secure nonpossessory, nonpurchase money loans may be the only means left to them to obtain needed funds. If true, one might expect to see the amount or frequency of loans secured with household goods remain unchanged. Controlling for changes, if any, in financial characteristics, the average debtor should borrow at the same level both pre- and post-BAPCPA. Alternatively, one might expect to see an increase in the amount and frequency of such loans if creditors became more willing to extend this type of credit now that the lien is less likely to be avoided in bankruptcy.

Has the Distribution of Debtors' Intentions Regarding Household Goods Pledged as Collateral for a Secured, Nonpossessory, Nonpurchase Money Loan Changed from Before to After BAPCPA Enactment?

A lien is a creditor's legal interest on the property that was pledged as collateral on a debt. A lien gives the creditor the right to repossess or force the sale of property if the debt is not paid. The debtor may seek to avoid a lien on exempt property. If the court approves the lien avoidance, the lien avoidance allows the debtor to keep the property and the debt behind the lien becomes an unsecured claim.[5] If a lien cannot be avoided, the debtor must redeem the property (pay the creditor the property's current replacement value or the outstanding balance on the loan, whichever is less), reaffirm the debt (agree on a repayment plan with the creditor), or surrender the property to the creditor. The limits introduced by BAPCPA on debtors' lien-avoidance rights on household goods may have reduced debtors' opportunities to avoid liens on their household goods and forced them either to repay nonpossesory, nonpurchase money loans secured by household goods or to surrender property that they would have been able to keep prior to BAPCPA. Debtors' plans as to their household goods that are collateral for nonpossessory, nonpurchase secured loans indicate the extent to which the changes in lien-avoidance rights introduced by BAPCPA have affected them.

---

[5] If the property is worth more than the legal exemption limit, the lien is reduced to the difference between the exemption limit and either the property's value or the amount of the debt, whichever is less.

Research Plan

There are two basic types of personal-bankruptcy filings:[6]

- liquidation under Chapter 7 of the Bankruptcy Code
- rehabilitation of the debtor under Chapter 13 of the Bankruptcy Code.

In our qualitative analyses, we sought the perceptions of individuals familiar with the bankruptcy system regarding the effects of the BAPCPA-introduced changes to lien-avoidance rights on Chapter 7 filers. Our quantitative analyses looked at data from Chapter 7 filings both before and after BAPCPA enactment to assess any changes in average amounts and frequency of liens on the narrowed category of household goods subject to lien avoidance and any differences in debtors' intents regarding the disposition of such liens. We did not evaluate Chapter 13 filings for two reasons. First, many Chapter 13 filings would not yet have an approved repayment plan when we drew the samples. The plans provide information on repayment of debts, including liens secured with household goods. Second, in Chapter 13, a debtor would still benefit from avoiding a lien, because the debt would now be unsecured and could be paid pro rata instead of in full. This is a smaller benefit, though, than the benefit that lien avoidance gives Chapter 7 debtors, who can effectively discharge the debt entirely and retain the property.

To elucidate issues and patterns, we conducted qualitative analyses based on interviews and group discussions with informed individuals and government employees involved in the bankruptcy process. We also conducted empirical analyses of samples of Chapter 7 bankruptcy cases filed in eight judicial districts across the country.

Qualitative Analyses

We interviewed 26 individuals who are involved in various aspects of the bankruptcy process (e.g., attorneys, trustees, creditors, consumer groups, judges) to get a broad view of how the changes in lien-avoidance rights introduced by BAPCPA are affecting debtors. Individuals were chosen from a variety of organizations. Interviews were conducted by telephone and were informed by a general interview guide developed by the research team. The interview guide highlighted the subjects to be covered during the discussion rather than giving a specific set of questions. Most individuals who participated had been working in the bankruptcy arena prior to the passage of BAPCPA. Therefore, they could provide insight into how the bankruptcy process has changed since the law was implemented and compare the old bankruptcy process to the current system. We did not interview debtors, as their information is limited to their own experience and is not necessarily generalizable to others' experiences or to how they might have fared pre-BAPCPA.

We also conducted group discussions with approximately 40 staff members, both analysts and attorneys, from four U.S. trustee (UST) regional offices at locations in various geographic areas. A protocol developed by the research team was used to guide the group discussions. However, the content and structure of the group discussions varied for each session.

---

[6] The Bankruptcy Code also provides for filings under Chapter 11, which allows a business or individuals with very high debt to pay debts while continuing to operate; and Chapter 12, which allows eligible family farmers and fishers to continue operations while reorganizing business affairs.

Bankruptcy Case Samples

Data on the characteristics of personal-bankruptcy cases are not available by judicial district. We asked EOUST's Office of Research and Planning to identify eight judicial districts that it considered representative of bankruptcy cases across the country. Based on its experience and knowledge of the various judicial districts, EOUST identified eight judicial districts that it believed offered a representative mix of urban and rural sites, size, relative frequency of Chapter 7 and Chapter 13 cases, and U.S.- versus foreign-born filers. Both before and after BAPCPA took effect, these eight districts accounted for approximately one-sixth of the individual bankruptcy cases across the country. These eight districts were thought to be fairly representative of all districts. We adopted these recommended districts as our sample districts. Table 1.1 lists the selected districts.

In consultation with EOUST, we determined that January 1, 2005, was a date sufficiently long before BAPCPA was enacted that cases filed on, or soon after that date, were not likely to reflect anticipation of the enactment of BAPCPA. We also determined that April 1, 2006, was a date sufficiently long after BAPCPA took effect that cases filed on, or soon after that date, were likely to reflect the effects of BAPCPA.

We drew the first 50 Chapter 7 cases filed in each of the selected districts on January 2, 2005, or immediately thereafter, in the order in which they were filed, that resulted in a discharge. We also drew the first 50 Chapter 7 cases filed in each of the selected districts on April 1, 2006, or immediately thereafter, in the order in which they were filed, that resulted in a discharge.

We drew only cases filed voluntarily by individuals, whether filing individually or jointly. We did not include involuntary filings or filings by entities other than individuals. We did not include cases that were dismissed or converted.

Organization of This Report

Chapter Two reviews the bankruptcy system. Chapter Three presents bankruptcy-system participants' perceptions of the effects of the change in debtors' lien-avoidance rights introduced by BAPCPA. Our empirical analyses of the case samples and the resulting estimates of the

Table 1.1
Judicial Districts Selected for Case Samples

Judicial District	UST Office
Eastern District of New York	Brooklyn and Central Islip
Western District of Texas	Austin and San Antonio
Western District of Tennessee	Memphis
Northern District of Ohio	Cleveland
Southern District of Iowa	Des Moines
Central District of California	Los Angeles, Riverside, Santa Ana, Woodland Hills
District of Utah	Salt Lake City
Middle District of Florida	Orlando and Tampa

effects of the use of these changes on debtors are presented in Chapter Four. Finally, Chapter Five summarizes our results and presents our conclusions.

The Bankruptcy System

The bankruptcy process is governed primarily by Title 11 of the U.S. Code, known as the Bankruptcy Code, and by the Federal Rules of Bankruptcy Procedure. There are two basic types of bankruptcy filings:

- liquidation under Chapter 7 of the Bankruptcy Code
- rehabilitation or reorganization of the debtor under chapters 11, 12, and 13 of the Bankruptcy Code.

Chapter 7 Bankruptcy

A Chapter 7 bankruptcy debtor receives a discharge of all dischargeable debt in return for turning over all of the debtor's nonexempt assets to a trustee.[1] A debtor may be denied a discharge only on specified grounds, including fraud committed in the bankruptcy process. Specific debts are statutorily nondischargeable (e.g., certain tax debts, alimony, child support).

A debtor may file for Chapter 7 relief without regard to the amount of the debtor's assets, liabilities, or degree of solvency. However, the Bankruptcy Code now contains the means test, a hurdle to filing based on the debtor's level of monthly disposable income (MDI). Individual debtors whose debts are primarily consumer debts are subject to the means test. A debtor can be barred from Chapter 7 protection if (1) his or her gross income exceeds the median income for his or her household size in the state of residence and (2) his or her MDI after allowed deductions exceeds statutory amounts, because the debtor is presumed to be able to repay his or her debts. It is the responsibility of the U.S. Trustee Program (USTP) to review the debtor's disposable income calculation under the means test. If USTP finds that a debtor fails the means test, USTP will ask the court to dismiss the case. The court determines whether a debtor qualifies for Chapter 7 protection.

If the trustee determines that there is nothing to be collected from the debtor and USTP determines that the means test is satisfied, then the case usually moves rapidly through the system and the debts are discharged. Historically, 70 percent of personal bankruptcies have been filed under Chapter 7.

---

[1] Although bankruptcies take place in the federal court system and follow federal law, state law may affect the property that a debtor may exempt (e.g., equity in a personal home and contents). Section 522 of the Bankruptcy Code provides that, unless a state opts out, a debtor may use a federal list of exemptions found in section 522(d). Most, but not all, states have opted out and established a list of exemptions. Debtors in certain states may elect to use federal exemptions instead of state ones. Thus, for example, a Texas debtor may choose either the state list or the federal list.

Chapter 11 Bankruptcy

Chapter 11 of the Bankruptcy Code allows individual debtors and business entities to pay debts while continuing to operate. A Chapter 11 debtor, often with the participation of creditors, creates a reorganization plan allowing repayment of all or part of the debt.

Chapter 12 Bankruptcy

Chapter 12 of the Bankruptcy Code allows eligible family farmers and fishers to file for bankruptcy, reorganize business affairs, continue operating, and repay all or part of the debts.

Chapter 13 Bankruptcy

Under Chapter 13 of the Bankruptcy Code, the debtor proposes a repayment plan that lasts three to five years. In return for monthly repayments to creditors, the debtor is permitted to retain all property, even that which a trustee would liquidate under Chapter 7. After court confirmation of the plan, a private trustee receives the payments from the debtor and makes distributions to creditors. Historically, 30 percent of personal bankruptcies have been Chapter 13 cases.

Bankruptcy Petitions and Schedules

Debtors under all chapters of the Bankruptcy Code are required to file, under oath, a petition, schedules of assets and liabilities, and a statement of financial affairs. This initial paperwork is the key to identifying the debtor's assets, debts, and income. The bankruptcy system is self-reporting, like the internal revenue system. The debtor is expected to list assets, debts, and income accurately and completely on the petition and schedules.

For this study, we focused on the lien-avoidance rights of Chapter 7 filers.

CHAPTER THREE

Participants' Perceptions of the Effects of the Changes in Debtor's Lien-Avoidance Rights

Overview

The data collection utilized discussion groups and interviews with individuals involved in various aspects of the bankruptcy process to collect qualitative data on the impact of the new definition of the types and quantities of personal property that constitute household goods for purposes of certain lien-avoidance actions. This data collection was meant to complement the quantitative analysis by providing detail and background information that could not be garnered from the bankruptcy cases. Specifically, the research team asked participants in the focus groups and interviews whether they had noticed any changes by businesses in their practices related to certain lien actions since BAPCPA enactment.

The team completed a total of 26 telephone interviews with assistant USTs and their staffs, Chapter 7 and Chapter 13 trustees, bankruptcy judges, academics, and representatives from consumer and credit groups. Many of the participants in the telephone interviews have played numerous roles in the bankruptcy process. For instance, interviews were conducted with both a judge and a law professor who formerly represented creditors. All of the individuals invited to participate in an interview had been working in the bankruptcy area prior to BAPCPA enactment. Therefore, they could provide insight into how the bankruptcy process has changed since the law was implemented and compare the old bankruptcy process to the current system. We did not interview individual debtors, as their information is limited to their own experience and not necessarily generalizable to other experiences or how they might have fared pre-BAPCPA. Additionally, we conducted group discussions with approximately 40 staff from four UST regional offices, including assistant USTs, staff attorneys, bankruptcy analysts, and paralegals.

The team selected Chapter 7 and Chapter 13 trustees and regional offices from the eight bankruptcy districts that were chosen in consultation with EOUST for the quantitative component of the study. For the individual interviews, we selected Chapter 7 and Chapter 13 trustees to represent a mix of urban and rural areas within those eight districts. The four UST regional offices used for the group discussions were selected to represent various geographic areas.

For the interviews, we developed a general interview guide that highlighted subjects to be covered, and the research team referred to the guide during the interviews. These interviews were not standardized, and the content and structure varied for each individual. A separate protocol was developed for the UST regional office group discussions (see the appendix).

Interview guides and group discussion protocols highlighted the following topics:

- changes by businesses in their practices since BAPCPA enactment, such as differences in the types of household goods used to secure nonpurchase money loans
- the effect that the changes in the narrowed category of household goods subject to lien avoidance has had on the bankruptcy courts
- whom the new law may affect.

Participants in the telephone interviews and group discussions had relatively little to say about these topics. The findings from the qualitative data collection are discussed below.

Change in Business Practices

Most participants believed either that this provision of the new law was not relevant for most debtors or that it was simply too soon to see an impact resulting from the changes. One Chapter 13 trustee noted that he had not seen the issue of nonpurchase money security on household goods come up once in more than 1,500 cases. Many echoed this, noting that one rarely sees nonpurchase money loans made using a household good as collateral. Although some commented that these types of loans were more prevalent 10 to 20 years ago, they have since significantly decreased. Most noted that they had not seen any impact from the new *household goods* definition on current cases and that the vast majority of loans secured with household goods involve purchase money security lending.

A law professor pointed out that, although *household goods* is more narrowly defined under BAPCPA, other categories are not defined. A debtor could therefore avoid a lien on a household good by moving it to a different category. One bankruptcy judge echoed this opinion when he described how the new law contains separate categories for items that might be thought of as the same thing (§522 and §522[f][4][1][b]). For example, household appliances could be listed as household goods or as appliances.

A potential concern with this new provision is that debtors might be coerced into unwise reaffirmation agreements in order to retain the exempt art, antiques, or jewelry now that they cannot avoid nonpossessory, nonpurchase money liens on these objects. One assistant UST indicated that he had seen more reaffirmation agreements on household goods recently, though it is not known whether this can be attributed to the revised definition of *household goods*.

Effect on the Courts

One bankruptcy judge did not believe that there has been any change due to the new definition of *household goods* and does not expect to see more cases related to this issue in the future. He noted that the cost of opposing the lien avoidance would be more than the value of the collateral. This thought was echoed by a Chapter 13 trustee, who noted that the law is open to interpretation (e.g., if a household has multiple TVs, which one is the exempt TV?). He felt that it would not be cost-effective to litigate these cases.

Whom the New Law May Affect

Some of the law professors noted that the new definition of *household goods* in the Bankruptcy Code was in line with the FTC Credit Practices Rule that has been in place since 1985 [16 CFR Section 444.1–444.5; definition of *household goods* is in section 444.1 I]. The FTC rule already prohibits nonpurchase money loans on items such as clothing and household goods. Therefore, one would not expect to see an impact on bankruptcy filings regarding such loans on household goods, since most such loans are illegal.

One attorney representing debtors noted that nonpurchase money loans secured with household goods are mainly obtained by poor rather than wealthy people. Since the poor are less likely to own art, antiques, jewelry, and expensive electronic entertainment equipment, the actual number of filings that this would affect is quite minimal. He also indicated that, over the past 15 years, lenders that make nonpurchase money loans on such household goods have been losing their market share to credit-card companies.

CHAPTER FOUR

Empirical Analyses of the Effects of the Changes in Debtors' Lien-Avoidance Rights

In this chapter, we attempt to quantitatively assess the effect of the narrowed category of household goods subject to lien avoidance that was introduced by BAPCPA. First, we discuss how we obtained our sample and the limitations on the information we could obtain. We then look at general characteristics of Chapter 7 debtors before and after BAPCPA enactment to determine whether there is a change in the type of debtor who is filing that may confound the effects we would observe from BAPCPA. We then look at effects that may have been introduced by BAPCPA's changes by examining the average amounts and frequency of liens on household goods subject to lien avoidance before and after BAPCPA enactment. We also look at similarities and differences in debtors' intents regarding the disposition of such liens.

Bankruptcy Case Samples

To support empirical analyses of the effects of changes in lien-avoidance rights that BAPCPA introduced, we drew samples of Chapter 7 cases and supporting schedules, hereafter referred to as *cases*. These cases were drawn from a representative set of bankruptcy-court districts across the country. We consulted with EOUST to select a set of districts in which filings are generally representative of bankruptcy filings across the country. Based on this consultation, we selected the eight districts listed in Table 1.1 in Chapter One.

Individual bankruptcy filings surged in September and October 2005 in anticipation of BAPCPA taking effect. Presumably, large numbers of individuals considering bankruptcy decided, or were advised by their attorneys, that they would fare better under the then-existing law than they would under the law as modified by BAPCPA. This raises the possibility that the pool of debtors filing for bankruptcy in the months immediately following BAPCPA's effective date might include disproportionate numbers of debtors whose bankruptcy case was not sensitive to the revisions introduced by BAPCPA. We thought that it might take some months before the pool of debtors filing for bankruptcy reflected the long-term, typical pool. We also thought that it might take some months for debtors and their advisors to become sufficiently familiar with BAPCPA that their filings reflected the effects of BAPCPA's provisions.

We wished to draw cases that had been filed sufficiently long after BAPCPA took effect that cases filed on, or after, that date are likely to reflect both the typical pool of debtors filing for bankruptcy and the effects of BAPCPA. However, a sizable fraction of cases are withdrawn, significantly modified, converted (from Chapter 7 to Chapter 13 or vice versa), or dismissed after they are filed. These changes are frequently caused by the discovery of errors in the original filing or by trustees' or bankruptcy-court judges' decisions regarding the appropriate disposition of the case. In these instances, some of the information that the debtor provided when the case was originally filed might have been erroneous. Accordingly, we thought it important to draw cases that had been filed sufficiently long before we drew them that we could reasonably expect that USTP analysts and trustees had reviewed the debtor-provided information and had not found any egregious errors.

In consultation with EOUST, we decided that April 1, 2006, was a date sufficiently long after BAPCPA took effect that cases filed on or soon after that date are likely to reflect the effects of BAPCPA on the typical pool of debtors filing for bankruptcy and will have been effectively completed by the time we began to draw the samples in November 2006.

We determined that cases filed under Chapter 7 on April 1, 2006, or soon after, were generally discharged, dismissed, or converted to Chapter 13 by the time we began to draw samples of cases in November 2006. A debtor who files under Chapter 7 must file a statement of intent that indicates his or her plan for the disposition of property that he or she owns that he or she has pledged as collateral for secured debts. The statement of intent must be completed soon after filing for bankruptcy and, if approved by the court, must be carried out. Accordingly, the information available for Chapter 7 cases filed on, or soon after, April 1, 2006, generally met our analysis needs.

A debtor who files under Chapter 13 must develop a plan for paying all, or a portion, of his or her debts, including secured debts, in up to five years. The development of a plan acceptable to the court may take several months. We drew samples of Chapter 13 cases filed on or soon after April 1, 2006, and observed that many of them had not developed an approved plan by the time we began to draw samples for this study. Further, a substantial fraction of Chapter 13 debtors do not complete their plans, and the ultimate disposition of the property they have pledged as collateral for a secured debt depends on the circumstances at the time.

Accordingly, we restricted our quantitative analyses to 16 samples of Chapter 7 cases (pre- and post-BAPCPA). We drew the first 50 Chapter 7 cases filed in each of the eight selected districts on January 2, 2005, or immediately thereafter, in the order in which they were filed, that resulted in a discharge. We drew the first 50 Chapter 7 cases filed in each of the eight selected districts on April 1, 2006, or immediately thereafter, in the order in which they were filed, that resulted in a discharge by December 8, 2006.

We drew only cases filed voluntarily by individuals, whether filing individually or jointly. We did not include involuntary filings or filings by entities other than individuals. We did not include dismissed or converted filings.

In total, we drew 400 cases pre-BAPCPA and 400 cases post-BAPCPA. After reviewing the data extracted from these cases, however, we dropped one pre-BAPCPA observation (Utah, case 05-20021). In this case, the amount listed as unsecured priority claims and total liabilities was significantly different from the other observations, and we believed it would exert undue influence over the analyses. The dropped observation had $20,533,419 and $21,893,560 listed as unsecured priority claims and total liabilities, respectively, whereas the next-highest amounts were $973,471 and $1,078,786, respectively. As a result, the analysis was conducted on a sample of 399 pre-BAPCPA cases and 400 post-BAPCPA cases.

Limitations on Information Contained in a Debtor's Bankruptcy Case

Although we initially believed that two samples each of 400 observations would be sufficient to detect significant differences, looking at the actual information we extracted, we discovered significant standard deviations for both samples due to wide variability in values listed on bankruptcy cases. As a result, the statistical power to detect significant differences is low for all of the general debtor financial characteristics.

We are similarly hampered with respect to BAPCPA-specific effects. To determine BAPCPA's effect on debtor and creditor behavior, we need to establish a baseline of how often debtors used those household goods now excluded from lien avoidance to secure nonpossessory loans before BAPCPA was enacted. Unfortunately, we cannot extract this exact information from the bankruptcy cases. The lien-avoidance changes in BAPCPA affected electronic equipment, works of art, and jewelry and antiques worth more than $500. (Hereafter, this set of household goods now excluded from lien avoidance due to BAPCPA will be referred to as *BAPCPA-affected goods*.) Unfortunately, Schedule B (a list of a debtor's personal property) does not contain specific line items for these goods. Similarly, Schedule D (a list of creditors holding secured claims) and the debtor's statement of intent do not designate whether the secured claim is possessory or nonpossessory.

Despite these limitations, we tried to form a general baseline using proxies. We used the general category of *household goods* (Schedule B, item 4) as a proxy for electronic equipment. For works of art and antiques, we used the general category of *collectibles* (Schedule B, item 5) as a proxy. And for jewelry, we used the joint *jewelry and furs* category (Schedule B, item 7). Finally, we also used the *other* personal-property category (Schedule B, item 33), in case a debtor included any BAPCPA-affected goods in this category.

Using these proxies, as demonstrated in Tables 4.1 and 4.2, such goods seldom have liens on them. The bankruptcy schedules do not distinguish between possessory and nonpossessory loans. However, it is likely that at least some of the liens on such goods are, in fact, possessory. Accordingly, the numbers presented in Tables 4.1 and 4.2 likely overstate the fraction of filings affected by BAPCPA. The sample size with which we are working regarding BAPCPA-specific changes is very small, with virtually no statistical power to detect differences.

Table 4.1
Loans Secured with BAPCPA-Affected Goods Prior to BAPCPA's Enactment

Type of Good	Filings with Secured Loans Pre-BAPCPA (n = 399)	Filings with Secured Loans Post-BAPCPA (n = 400)
Household goods	32	39
Collectibles	0	0
Jewelry and furs	3	2
Other	2	3
Total number of filings with secured loans[a]	36	42

[a] Some cases have loans secured with more than one type of BAPCPA-affected goods. As a result, pre-BAPCPA, there are 37 loans secured by BAPCPA-related goods but only 36 filings with such loans. Post-BAPCPA, there are 44 loans secured by BAPCPA-affected goods but only 42 filings with such loans.

Table 4.2
Chapter 7 Cases with Liens on BAPCPA-Affected Goods Before and After BAPCPA Enactment

Type of Good	Cases with Liens Pre-BAPCPA (%)	Cases with Liens Post-BAPCPA (%)
All BAPCPA-affected goods	9.0	10.5

General Debtor Financial Characteristics

We evaluated debtors' financial characteristics before and after BAPCPA enactment to look for differences and trends in debtor type or composition that may confound BAPCPA's effects, recognizing that the low statistical power may inhibit our ability to draw specific conclusions regarding any variations we may observe.

From the Chapter 7 cases we reviewed, we extracted information for each debtor regarding total personal property, total secured claims, total unsecured priority claims, total unsecured nonpriority claims, current monthly income, current monthly expenditures, total assets, and total liabilities. We also extracted information on BAPCPA-related goods using the proxies discussed previously.

To determine differences pre- and post-BAPCPA, we looked at both the mean and median of the data. For the mean, we conducted unpaired, two-sided t-tests, using a p-value of 0.05 to determine significance. For the median, we used an unpaired median test (which indicates whether the two samples are significantly different in their distribution) with a p-value of 0.05 to determine significance.

There were no significant differences in either the mean or median with respect to basic financial characteristics such as monthly income, monthly expenses, assets, or liabilities. Table 4.3 presents the findings with respect to differences in the mean, or average Chapter 7 debtor.

Even though there were no significant differences, we do see a notable downward trend in both total assets and liabilities. To explore this change further, we looked at individual assets and liabilities but similarly found no significant difference in either the mean or median, as set forth in Table 4.4.

Although there is no significant difference in any category, it does appear that the change in assets and liabilities is being driven by a drop in average real property values as well as a corresponding drop in the average secured-claim amount. It may be that these declines represent a real change that cannot be statistically captured due to the wide variation in the values, especially for the pre-BAPCPA filings. If it is a true decline, the change appears to be from a decline in actual value, as the number of debtors who had real-property assets and secured claims remained stable.

Table 4.3
Debtors' General Financial Characteristics Pre- and Post-BAPCPA Enactment

Characteristic	Average Pre-BAPCPA ($) (n = 399)	Average Post-BAPCPA ($) (n = 400)	p-value
Monthly income	2,050	1,882	0.21
Monthly expenses	2,337	2,239	0.37
Total assets	62,609	52,812	0.13
Total liabilities	107,070	91,162	0.08

Table 4.4
Average Value of Debtors' Individual Assets and Liabilities Pre- and Post-BAPCPA Enactment

Characteristic	Average Pre-BAPCPA	Average Post-BAPCPA	p-value
Assets			
Personal property	$16,125 (n = 399)	$15,992 (n = 400)	0.95
Real property	$46,481 (n = 154)	$36,870 (n = 153)	0.10
Liabilities			
Secured claims	$52,495 (n = 247)	$41,063 (n = 242)	0.10
Unsecured priority	$1,748 (n = 78)	$1,707 (n = 61)	0.94
Unsecured nonpriority	$52,825 (n = 399)	$47,395 (n = 400)	0.29

To further explore this change, we looked at the distribution of real-property and secured claims and found that there was no indication of any changes other than those noted previously. The distribution findings are listed in Table 4.5.

In addition to looking at the mean and median values, we also looked at the mix of assets and liabilities. To do so, for each individual debtor, we calculated the specific asset or liability as a percentage of the debtor's total assets or liabilities. We then looked at the mean mix but found no significant difference. Table 4.6 presents these findings.

The mix of assets and liabilities for the average debtor remained stable, with about 30 percent of assets in real property and 70 percent in personal property and about 31 percent of liabilities in secured claims and about 69 percent in unsecured claims. For BAPCPA-affected goods, there was no significant difference in the mean or median with respect to the value of such goods or their average mix[1] as a percentage of personal property. These findings are listed in Tables 4.7 and 4.8, respectively.

Table 4.5
Distribution of Debtors' Real-Property and Secured Claims

	Pre-BAPCPA ($) (n = 399)			Post-BAPCPA ($) (n = 400)		
Characteristic	25th Percentile	Median	75th Percentile	25th Percentile	Median	75th Percentile
Real property	0	0	75,000	0	0	65,000
Secured claims	0	8,500	74,277	0	6,494	67,017

NOTE: To calculate the percentiles, the cases were ordered from lowest to highest, and the specified percentile represents the individual debtor's value at that point. It is not an average.

---

[1] To calculate the mix, we used the same process described in the "General Debtor Financial Characteristics" section of this report.

Table 4.6
Average Debtor's Mix of Assets and Liabilities

Characteristic	Average Pre-BAPCPA (%) (n = 399)	Average Post-BAPCPA (%) (n = 400)	p-value
Assets			
Real property/total assets	31.7	29.4	0.44
Personal property/total assets	68.3	70.6	0.45
Liabilities			
Secured claims/total liabilities	31.4	30.5	0.7
Unsecured priority/total liabilities	2.2	2.2	0.92
Unsecured nonpriority/total liabilities	66.4	67.3	0.71

Table 4.7
Average Value of BAPCPA-Affected Goods

Characteristic	Average Pre-BAPCPA ($) (n = 399)	Average Post-BAPCPA ($) (n = 400)	p-value
Household goods	1,209	1,336	0.17
Collectibles	51	75	0.56
Jewelry and furs	209	189	0.71
Other	30	30	0.99

Table 4.8
Average Mix of BAPCPA-Affected Goods as a Percentage of Debtors' Personal Property

Characteristic	Average Pre-BAPCPA (%) (n = 399)	Average Post-BAPCPA (%) (n = 400)	p-value
Household good/personal property	18.0	21.0	0.37
Collectibles/personal property	0.7	0.9	0.26
Jewelry and furs/personal property	1.7	2.1	0.29

With respect to ownership rates, we could not determine whether there was a change in the number of debtors who owned excess electronic equipment. This type of property is lumped in with other household goods such as furnishings, and almost all debtors, both pre- and post-BAPCPA, owned some form of these items. But Table 4.9 sets forth actual ownership rates of other BAPCPA-affected goods using the proxies discussed previously.

With respect to jewelry worth in excess of $500 (using the joint category of jewelry and furs as a proxy), we found no significant change, as ownership remained stable at about 8 percent of the filings. Similarly, there was no change in rates of ownership of other personal property, as it remained stable at about 6 percent of all Chapter 7 filings. But we did find a significant increase in the number of debtors who owned collectibles, which would include works of art, and antiques worth more than $500. Pre-BAPCPA, 26 percent of those filing owned such items, while, post-BAPCPA, 33 percent did. However, the impact of this change on the

Table 4.9
Chapter 7 Debtors Who Owned BAPCPA-Affected Goods

Characteristic	Pre-BAPCPA	Post-BAPCPA	p-value
Collectible ownership	25.8% (n = 103)	33.3% (n = 133)	0.02
Jewelry and furs worth >$500	8.0% (n = 32)	9.0% (n = 36)	0.6
Other ownership	5.8% (n = 23)	5.5% (n = 22)	0.88

financial condition of the average debtor is negligible, given that collectibles represent less than 1 percent of their total personal property.

Loans Secured with Household Goods

Part of the motivation behind BAPCPA was a perception that debtors were using their household goods as security to obtain loans that they never intended to repay. Instead, debtors filed for bankruptcy and used the nonpossessory, nonpurchase money lien avoidance to avoid the liens, reducing the claims to unsecured debt. If true, we would expect a reduction in the amount and frequency of secured loans on BAPCPA-affected goods as BAPCPA significantly limited debtors' incentive to engage in this behavior.

Another possibility, however, is that debtors are motivated by need rather than by the potential benefits of the bankruptcy provisions. Under this scenario, debtors do not use BAPCPA-affected goods to obtain loans because they think the lien can be avoided in a subsequent bankruptcy, but because it is the only means left to them to obtain funds. If true, one might expect to see the amount or frequency of loans secured with BAPCPA-affected goods to remain unchanged. Assuming that the financial characteristics of the average Chapter 7 debtor did not significantly change, he or she would borrow at the same level both pre- and post-BAPCPA. Alternatively, one might expect to see an increase in the amount and frequency of such loans if creditors became more willing to extend this type of credit now that the lien is less likely to be avoided in bankruptcy. Table 4.10 shows the average amount and frequency of loans secured by household goods that would be affected by the BAPCPA changes.

From the data we have, we found a slight decrease in the average amount of loans secured with household goods that would be affected by the BAPCPA changes but an increase in the frequency of such loans. In other words, a few more debtors obtained loans secured with BAPCPA-affected goods, but the amount of loans that each debtor received, on average, declined. This decline in the average amount of secured loans on BAPCPA-affected goods is in line with an overall downward trend in the average for all secured-claim amounts. But these changes were

Table 4.10
Amount and Frequency of Loans Secured with Household Goods

Loans Secured by Household Goods	Pre-BAPCPA Mean	Post-BAPCPA Mean	p-value
Amount	$3,884	$2,810	0.18
Frequency	9.0% (n = 36)	10.5% (n = 42)	0.48

NOTE: Total filings pre-BAPCPA: n = 399. Total filings post-BAPCPA: n = 400.

not significant. And, given the extremely small sample size of the number of loans secured with BAPCPA-affected goods, it is impossible to make any conclusions regarding these changes.

Debtors' Intentions Regarding the Disposition of Secured Debts

A lien is a creditor's legal claim on the property that was pledged as collateral on a debt. A lien gives the creditor the right to repossess or force the sale of property if the debt is not paid. But with respect to nonpossessory, nonpurchase liens, the debtor may seek to avoid them if they are on exempt property. If approved by the court, the debtor keeps the property and the debt behind the lien becomes an unsecured claim. If a lien cannot be avoided, the debtor must redeem the property (pay the creditor the property's current replacement value or the outstanding balance on the loan, whichever is less), reaffirm the debt (agree on a repayment plan with the creditor), or surrender the property to the creditor. The limits on debtors' lien-avoidance rights under BAPCPA may have reduced debtors' opportunities to avoid liens on certain goods and forced them to either repay or surrender property that they would have been able to keep prior to BAPCPA enactment. As a result, we looked at debtors' intentions regarding the disposition of liens secured with BAPCPA-affected goods as an indication of the extent to which they have been affected by the changes in lien-avoidance rights BAPCPA introduced.

Unfortunately, there were so few filings that had an actual secured claim against household goods (about 10 percent of the filings) that we could not conduct any meaningful statistical analysis of the differences in debtors' intentions regarding the claims. But Table 4.11 sets forth the actual distribution of debtors' intentions for those few filings that did include a secured claim against household goods.

Although there is an insufficient number of observations to determine any statistically significant differences, these figures still provide some insight into BAPCPA's effect. First, fewer than 10 percent of Chapter 7 debtors pre-BAPCPA entered bankruptcy with secured claims against BAPCPA-affected goods, and, of those who did, very few attempted to avoid the lien through a property exemption. Rather, in the main, the debtors either surrendered the goods to the creditor or reaffirmed the loan. And as some, if not most, of these secured loans were probably possessory liens, the use of the nonpossessory, nonpurchase lien provision seems to be extremely rare, undermining the assertion about widespread debtor abuse of the nonpossessory, nonpurchase lien-avoidance provision before BAPCPA.

Table 4.11
Debtors' Intentions Regarding Secured Claims on Household Goods

Debtors' Intention	Pre-BAPCPA		Post-BAPCPA	
	Claims	Percent of Total	Claims	Percent of Total
Surrender	12	34	10	24
Exempt	3	9	3	7
Redeem	3	9	5	12
Reaffirm	17	49	18	44
Combination	0	0	5	12
Total	35		41	

NOTE: Percentages subject to rounding.

With respect to the post-BAPCPA figures, the most interesting change is in the increase in what we have termed *combination* intentions. In these cases, debtors listed an intention to exempt *and* some other intention such as surrender.[2] It could be that this is simply an error. Alternatively, since BAPCPA-affected goods are usually not individually listed but lumped in together with other property, it could be that debtors intend to exempt some of the goods and surrender or reaffirm others. If the latter explanation is true, it might reflect BAPCPA's limitation on lien avoidance, in that now debtors have to surrender or reaffirm certain household goods that they otherwise would have exempted. Unfortunately, given the small numbers of such intentions in our data set, it is impossible to test the validity of this hypothesis.

---

[2]   Of the five "combination" cases, two listed exempt and surrender, one listed exempt and reaffirm, one listed exempt and redeem, and one listed surrender and reaffirm.

CHAPTER FIVE

Conclusions

It is impossible to draw any conclusions regarding BAPCPA's effect on debtors' lien-avoidance rights. Qualitative interviews indicated that there was no impact, but, unfortunately, we could not conduct any meaningful statistical analysis to examine the qualitative findings more rigorously. We had an overall sample size of 799 (399 pre-BAPCPA and 400 post-BAPCPA), but the number of filings with loans potentially secured by BAPCPA-affected goods was small—36 pre-BAPCPA and 42 post-BAPCPA. Moreover, the bankruptcy schedules do not contain sufficient detail to determine whether the goods involved were actually affected by BAPCPA's changes or whether the loans were possessory or nonpossessory. As a result, statistical analysis regarding BAPCPA's impact was not feasible. Based on our sample, the only conclusion we can make is that, even before BAPCPA enactment, few debtors used BAPCPA-affected goods to secure loans (about 10 percent) and that, of those, even fewer attempted to avoid the lien by claiming an exemption (fewer than 1 percent).[1]

It should be noted that this study does not attempt to test whether BAPCPA has accomplished its intended goals. For example, the lien-avoidance limitations in BAPCPA may have been designed to address a very small minority of wealthy debtors who engage in big-ticket abuse of the provision. If so, future research on whether the provision reduced this abuse will be challenged by the inherent difficulty in identifying a sufficiently large number of qualifying debtors. Studying other possible effects such as improved consistency of court decisions and reduced litigation will also require a substantially different study design focused on a much more restrictive segment of the debtor population.

In sum, from both the qualitative and quantitative analyses, it appears that Chapter 7 debtors in our samples rarely, if ever, availed themselves of the nonpossessory, nonpurchase lien-avoidance provision even before or since BAPCPA took effect. As most Chapter 7 debtors do not even own items on which a nonpossessory, nonpurchase security interest is legal (works of art, jewelry other than wedding rings, and antiques), the limited use of such liens is not surprising. Consequently, determining BAPCPA's impact will require follow-up research using an extremely large sample size of bankruptcy cases.

---

[1] And since the cases do not indicate under what provision the debtor was claiming the exemption, we cannot even say for certain whether *any* debtor in our sample actually availed himself or herself of the nonpossessory, nonpurchase lien exemption prior to BAPCPA enactment.

Group Discussion Guide

1. Have you noticed any changes by businesses in their practices since BAPCPA? For instance, have you seen a difference in the type of household goods used to secure the claims? Have you seen liens against household goods that are no longer exempt?
2. Have you seen a difference in the total amount and/or number of claims against the debtor that are secured by household goods?
3. What effect, if any, do you think the changes in the exemptions on household goods have had on the bankruptcy courts? (More motions? Fewer motions?)
4. Who do you think this change is affecting? Why was this change made to the law?
5. Do you know of any companies that extend credit by using household goods to secure the claim?
6. Are you aware of the FTC law affecting loans on household goods?

References

Code of Federal Regulations, Title 16, Part 444.1 et seq., Credit Practices.

Public Law 109-8, Bankruptcy Abuse Prevention and Consumer Protection Act of 2005, April 20, 2005.